LIVE BETTER

A BOOK OF
SPIRITUAL GUIDANCE

SOPHIE GOLDING

LIVE BETTER

Copyright © Summersdale Publishers Ltd, 2017

Images © Shutterstock

With research by Vicki Vrint

Design by Luci Ward

Vie Books is an imprint of Summersdale Publishers Ltd

Summersdale Publishers Ltd
46 West Street
Chichester
West Sussex
PO19 1RP
UK

www.summersdale.com

Printed and bound in Croatia

ISBN: 978-1-84953-988-3

Substantial discounts on bulk quantities of Summersdale books are available to corporations, professional associations and other organisations. For details contact general enquiries: telephone: +44 (0) 1243 771107, fax: +44 (0) 1243 786300 or email: enquiries@summersdale.com.

CONTENTS

INTRODUCTION

The benefits of living a spiritual lifestyle are enormous. A spiritual life will bring you peace and happiness; it will teach you how to handle difficult situations with a calm and considered approach; it will help you to discover what is truly important to you and give you the confidence to reach your goals. You will no longer regard challenges as obstacles and you will come to understand that the answers you seek are already within you.

This book shows you how to start your spiritual journey, drawing together wisdom from the world's greatest traditions, which have guided and inspired people for centuries. By exploring these different ideas and philosophies, you will discover which principles ring true for you. Each section includes practical tips for you to try, which will help you to incorporate spirituality into your everyday life, discover new ways of thinking and increase your self-awareness.

Setting aside a little time to try out these simple techniques will bring you huge rewards, from your new attitude of positivity and compassion, to a greater connection with the world around you and your spiritual self. You'll live a happier, healthier and more authentic life. You'll live *better*, and that's the best reward of all.

MINDFULNESS

Mindfulness involves focusing on the sensations of the present moment to find an oasis of mental peace, away from the stresses of everyday life. Based on Buddhist teachings, it shows us how to take a step back and look at our lives with an attitude of acceptance and compassion.

Many of us rush through our days on autopilot, completing task after task without paying much attention to what we are doing. But if you simply pause for a moment, focus on your breathing and then concentrate fully on the task at hand, you'll stop your mind from flitting from one thing to the next. This will automatically make you feel more centred. You'll be able to observe your activities and thoughts in a detached and calm way. (With a little practice you can learn to handle challenging situations with a moment of mindful consideration – it's a very useful skill to have!)

Incorporating mindfulness into your daily life is a great way to start your spiritual journey. You may decide to set aside time every day to achieve mindfulness through meditation, but it can also be practised less formally, whenever or wherever you like. Try it now: take a few moments to pay attention to the sounds around you, and the texture and weight of this book in your hands. You'll feel calmer instantly.

EMBRACE THE EVERYDAY

Start to practise mindfulness by picking an everyday task and carrying it out in a mindful manner. Choose something mundane that you usually do without thinking, such as cleaning your teeth, washing the dishes or doing your weekly shop. Take time to focus on your task completely: notice the taste of your toothpaste, the temperature of the water or the colours of the fruit on display. You'll not only feel calmer, you'll also find that you're more effective at what you're doing.

CHANGING THE WAY YOU
DO ROUTINE THINGS
ALLOWS A NEW PERSON
TO GROW INSIDE OF YOU.

Paulo Coelho

BE CREATIVE

By learning to celebrate your senses – smell, touch, sight, hearing and taste – you'll give your brain a well-earned rest from multi-tasking. Many people find that becoming absorbed in a creative pursuit, such as colouring, can help them to focus in this way. There are plenty of books and apps available, which combine colouring with gentle mindfulness exercises, to get you started.

ENGAGE WITH THE MOMENT

Paying attention to your surroundings helps you to slow down and experience life in the 'now'. Instead of dwelling on the past or worrying about the future, steady your thoughts and focus on the details of the present moment. The past has gone forever and the future hasn't yet arrived, so gently push aside any worries you have about them and remind yourself that *in this moment* you are safe and all is well.

THERE'S NO
PAST AND THERE'S NO
FUTURE. ALL THERE
IS, EVER, IS THE NOW.

George Harrison

BECOME AN OBSERVER

Practise mindfulness the next time you encounter a stressful situation or challenging emotion. Once you're feeling grounded in the present, consider your problem as if you were an uninvolved observer, rather than the person at the centre of the situation. You'll be able to get a little perspective and respond in a much more balanced way.

MEDITATION

The word 'meditation' comes from the Latin *meditari* (to think, dwell on, exercise the mind) and *mederi*, to heal. At its simplest, it involves taking time out to sit still, away from distractions, and clear the mind of everyday thoughts. It allows us to take a break from 'doing' and to spend time simply 'being' instead, giving our minds a rest and a chance to recover from the rigours of everyday life.

Meditation forms an integral part of many ancient spiritual practices, but it is as relevant to us today as it has ever been. The benefits are enormous: on the physical side, it lowers blood pressure and boosts the immune system, while on the emotional side, it helps us to combat stress. Setting aside time to meditate also allows us to nurture our spirituality.

Anyone can learn to meditate. Start small: find a quiet place to sit for a few minutes, minimise any distractions and focus on your breathing. With practice you'll find it easier to meditate for longer periods of time.

If the idea of sitting in complete silence seems a little off-putting at first, try a guided meditation: an audio track that will talk you through a simple visualisation. (This is perfect if you're new to meditating.) Some guided meditations will even help you to explore a specific issue, such as stress management or building self-confidence.

TRUE SPIRITUALITY
IS A MENTAL ATTITUDE
YOU CAN PRACTISE
AT ANY TIME.

Dalai Lama

SEEK SANCTUARY

Find a place of personal sanctuary – anything from a comfortable chair in the corner of your bedroom to a tranquil spot high upon a hill – and make time to visit it and meditate as often as you can. Away from distractions, you'll find it easier to clear your mind and nurture your spirituality.

ESTABLISH A ROUTINE

If you can, aim to set aside 15 minutes a day to meditate. Try to do it at the same time every day and establish a routine as you make your meditation space ready: for example, turn off your phone, close the door and arrange your cushions. This will train your brain to slow down and enter a more peaceful state of mind. Then sit quietly with your eyes closed. Focus on your breathing and the sounds around you, rather than your thoughts.

QUIET
YOUR MIND

If you find everyday thoughts clamouring for your attention – and they will at first – acknowledge them and then allow them to drift away. Remember that you have the power to control your thoughts. Don't be downhearted if you feel that a meditation session hasn't gone to plan. There is no 'right' or 'wrong' way to do it, and giving yourself time out is always a positive thing to do.

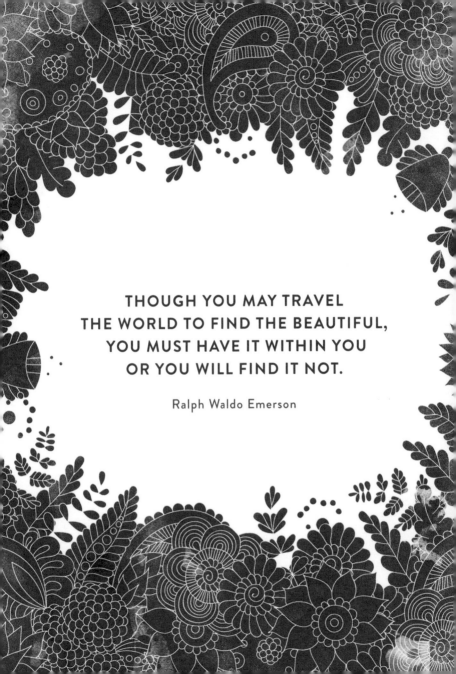

THOUGH YOU MAY TRAVEL
THE WORLD TO FIND THE BEAUTIFUL,
YOU MUST HAVE IT WITHIN YOU
OR YOU WILL FIND IT NOT.

Ralph Waldo Emerson

TRUST YOUR SPIRITUAL SELF

Meditation allows us to explore our spirituality. In days gone by, spirituality was connected to organised religion but for many people nowadays it is more about personal development. When we grow spiritually, we learn to listen to our inner voice, to live in love and positivity, and to become more conscious of our inner being. Your spirituality stays with you no matter what – learn to trust it and you can handle whatever life throws your way.

YOGA

Yoga is a Sanskrit word meaning 'to join or unite'. It generally refers to the union between soul and body, and is a practice that can form part of any belief system, although it has its roots in Hindu teachings. Many of us in the Western world are familiar with yoga as a form of physical exercise, but it has a deeply spiritual element too. It is a holistic system, balancing the mind, body and spirit.

Hatha (or active) yoga is the most common type practised in the West. It combines various strengthening postures and stretches with breathing and meditation exercises, and its benefits include increased flexibility and relaxation, as well as relief from stress and pain. There are many different styles of hatha yoga, with different emphases on posture, meditation and yogic breathing.

Yoga's popularity means that there is a mass of information available for the beginner: there are countless websites, books, magazines and groups devoted to its practice. It's also very easy to make yoga a part of your life. A good starting point is a beginners' class, where you can learn some basic postures and breathing techniques. You'll come away with ideas for simple poses and meditations that you can practise at home.

Making yoga a part of your daily routine – even if it's something as simple as a relaxation exercise – will enhance your well-being.

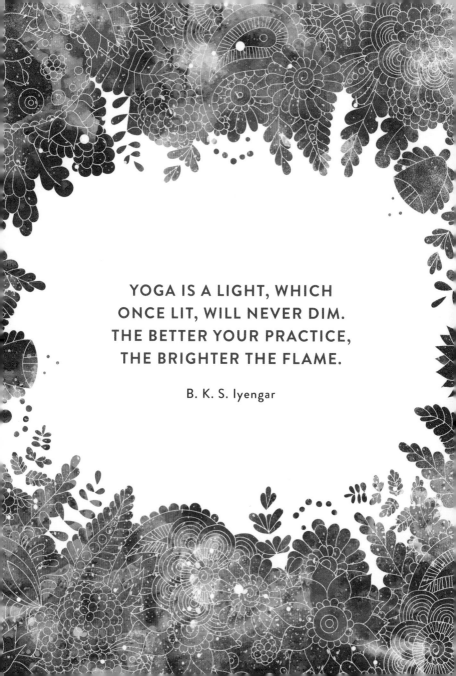

YOGA IS A LIGHT, WHICH
ONCE LIT, WILL NEVER DIM.
THE BETTER YOUR PRACTICE,
THE BRIGHTER THE FLAME.

B. K. S. Iyengar

FIND A GURU

Whether you track down a local class or try out some one-to-one lessons, getting guidance from someone you trust is the best place to start. In life we often feel that it's down to us to solve everything ourselves, but learning to take advice from others is a good skill to develop. Many qualities we cultivate in yoga, such as balance, concentration and perseverance, are useful in other areas of our lives, too.

A PATH TO PROGRESS

Like yoga, spirituality is a practice that can be learned, developed and applied. Attending a weekly yoga class can give you the opportunity for a spiritual workout, as well as a physical one, as it allows you time to reflect and tune in to your inner self. By practising regularly, you will give yourself the chance to continue your spiritual journey.

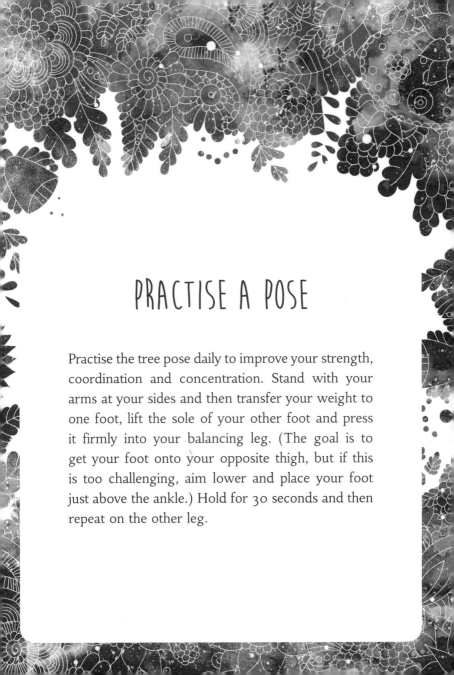

PRACTISE A POSE

Practise the tree pose daily to improve your strength, coordination and concentration. Stand with your arms at your sides and then transfer your weight to one foot, lift the sole of your other foot and press it firmly into your balancing leg. (The goal is to get your foot onto your opposite thigh, but if this is too challenging, aim lower and place your foot just above the ankle.) Hold for 30 seconds and then repeat on the other leg.

KNOWING YOURSELF
IS THE BEGINNING
OF ALL WISDOM.

Aristotle

RELAX AND RELEASE

Most yoga classes finish with a relaxation exercise. Try this after a stressful day: lie on your back with your arms stretched out by your sides. Close your eyes and breathe slowly and deeply. Focus on relaxing each part of your body in turn, from your head down to your feet. At each stage, release any tension and imagine yourself sinking into the floor beneath you. Finish by gently moving your fingers and toes before opening your eyes.

YOGIC BREATHING

Yogic breathing, or *pranayama*, lies at the heart of yoga practice. Defined as the control of life force, it increases vital energy in the body, and calms and steadies the mind. Other benefits include improved digestion and sleep; also, since focusing on breathing helps us to achieve mindfulness, yogic breathing is a route to all the benefits of mindfulness and meditation.

There are many different yogic breathing techniques, each with a different focus, but making any effort to deepen your breathing will be beneficial, as you'll be providing your body with a better supply of oxygen. Most of us rarely think about the way we breathe and use only 50 per cent of our lung capacity, snatching shallow breaths into the top of our lungs. Practise breathing from the diaphragm whenever you can and you'll feel instantly re-energised.

Sit in a comfortable position with your shoulders slightly back to open up your chest. Placing your hand on your stomach, exhale through the mouth and inhale deeply and slowly through the nose, feeling your hand rise and fall with each breath. Once you've mastered this simple exercise and felt the benefits, you can move on to explore different breathing techniques (for cleansing, relaxation, combatting stress, etc.). Internet tutorials are excellent for this – you can even fit a little yogic breathing into your lunch break.

RELAX WITH BRAHMARI

Making time to focus on your breathing at least once a day will leave you feeling calmer. Try the humming bee breath *(brahmari)* every night before you go to bed, for example. Sit comfortably with your back straight, use the tips of your index fingers to block your ears and then inhale deeply through your nose. As you exhale through your nose, hum continuously and feel the sound vibrate through your throat and head. Repeat until you feel truly relaxed.

START BY DOING WHAT'S
NECESSARY, THEN DO
WHAT'S POSSIBLE;
AND SUDDENLY YOU ARE
DOING THE IMPOSSIBLE.

St Francis of Assisi

REAL PEACE IS
UNSHAKEABLE.
BLISS IS
UNCHANGED BY
GAIN OR LOSS.

Yogi Bhajan

LEARN TO BREATHE DEEPLY

When we have a shock or receive bad news, we often gasp or hold our breath. This sudden, short inhalation triggers our fight-or-flight response, setting our hearts racing and making adrenalin pump around the body. Learn to combat this stress response with some deep, slow breaths and you'll be able to remain calm and breathe through those tricky moments.

CHANTING

Chanting – the rhythmic repetition of sounds or phrases – is a common way of connecting with the spiritual and is an integral part of many religious practices, from Buddhist throat-singing to the uplifting mantras of Hindu tradition. By focusing on chanting a simple phrase, the mind is set free from everyday thoughts and able to reach a higher state of consciousness.

Chanting is a powerful preparation for meditation and provides us with many of the same benefits, including relaxing the mind and body, and heightening our energy and concentration levels. Chanting (or singing of any kind) allows us to release negative emotions that we may be harbouring and to avoid mental or emotional blockages.

When we chant, we are listening to the sound as well as producing it, which is why the mantras we choose can be so powerful. By repeating a simple inspirational phrase, such as 'I am happy' or 'All is well', we can train our minds to take a more positive approach to ourselves and life in general.

Search online for examples of chanting and give it a try. Chanting with others certainly magnifies the benefits and an Internet search will reveal any classes or chanting groups near you. You can also benefit from chanting alone, though. Use it as a tool to help you on your spiritual journey: to aid meditation, release negative emotions or reinforce positive thoughts.

DANCE AND SING IT OUT

Bring music into your life and joy will come with it. Dance, sing and laugh as often as you possibly can. Remember what it was like to be a child, when unselfconsciousness and spontaneity ruled. Sometimes, as adults, we are afraid to show or feel happiness. Aspire to express yourself through music.

**CHANTING OPENS
THE HEART AND MAKES
LOVE FLOW WITHIN US.**

Muktananda

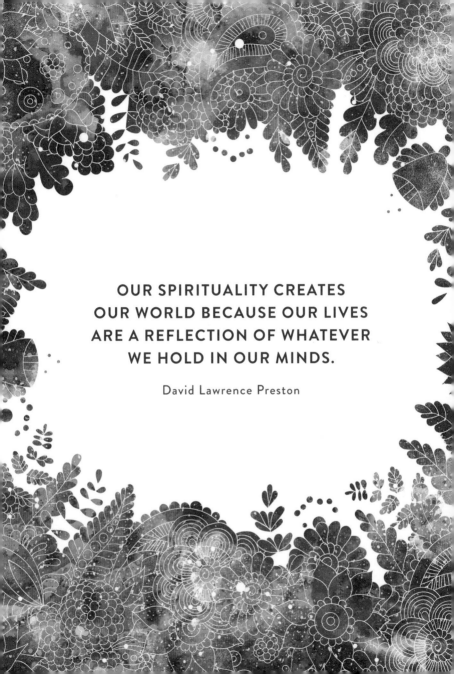

OUR SPIRITUALITY CREATES
OUR WORLD BECAUSE OUR LIVES
ARE A REFLECTION OF WHATEVER
WE HOLD IN OUR MINDS.

David Lawrence Preston

PICK A POWER MANTRA

Create your own happiness mantra: stand in front of a mirror and repeat a positive statement about yourself in the present tense, such as 'I am prosperous', 'I am calm' or 'I love myself no matter what'. Try to do this every day for three weeks and you will find that you start to feel better about yourself.

LU JONG

This form of yoga was originally practised by Buddhist monks in Tibet. Isolated from medical help in their mountain monasteries, they developed a series of moves and breathing exercises to maintain physical health, address common ailments and balance the mind. The Tibetan words *lu jong* mean 'body transformation' and the focus of this practice is on healing.

Buddhists (and many others) believe that physical ailments and emotional upsets are the result of blockages in the channels that allow energy to flow around our bodies. By gently applying pressure to specific points throughout the body, Lu Jong releases blockages and corrects any resulting imbalance. Spinal health is key to Lu Jong: the spine is seen as the 'energy box' of the body, and the exercises focus on developing spinal strength and good posture.

Lu Jong is based on balancing the five elements of the universe – space, earth, wind, fire and water – within the body. Tibetan monks observed that the balance of these elements changes throughout the day and identified ways in which we can work in harmony with them at these times.

The four groups of Lu Jong movements flow on from one another and should be practised in strict order. The best place to start is a beginners' course, which will introduce you to the first group of moves – the Five Elements. Although Lu Jong classes may be tricky to track down, there are some great online resources.

LET YOUR BODY
BE YOUR GUIDE

An important aspect of Lu Jong is developing body awareness. Listen to your body and let your energy guide you to choose the best time of day to practise yoga or meditation. Some people find that early morning works best for them, while others feel better able to relax in the evening. You may find that your practice time will differ depending on the season, too.

MOVEMENT IS A MEDICINE
FOR CREATING CHANGE
IN A PERSON'S PHYSICAL,
EMOTIONAL AND
MENTAL STATE.

Carol Welch-Baril

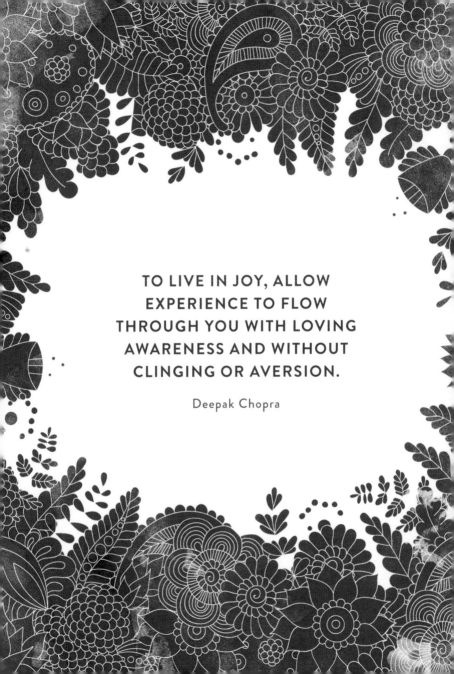

TO LIVE IN JOY, ALLOW
EXPERIENCE TO FLOW
THROUGH YOU WITH LOVING
AWARENESS AND WITHOUT
CLINGING OR AVERSION.

Deepak Chopra

DISCOVER YOUR PRESSURE POINTS

Gentle pressure on points throughout the body can help us to clear blockages in our energy channels and relieve stress. If you are feeling anxious, try applying gentle pressure to the 'inner gate' – a point three finger-widths down from your wrist – and you'll instantly feel more relaxed. For an energy boost, massage the webbing between your thumb and index finger of each hand.

TAKE A HOLISTIC APPROACH

Be aware that you are a spiritual being in a physical body – and remember that your physical, emotional and spiritual aspects are all linked. A blockage in one aspect of our lives can lead to symptoms on other levels. By practising Lu Jong, or any form of holistic therapy, we are not simply taking care of ourselves physically, but also tending to our emotional and spiritual health.

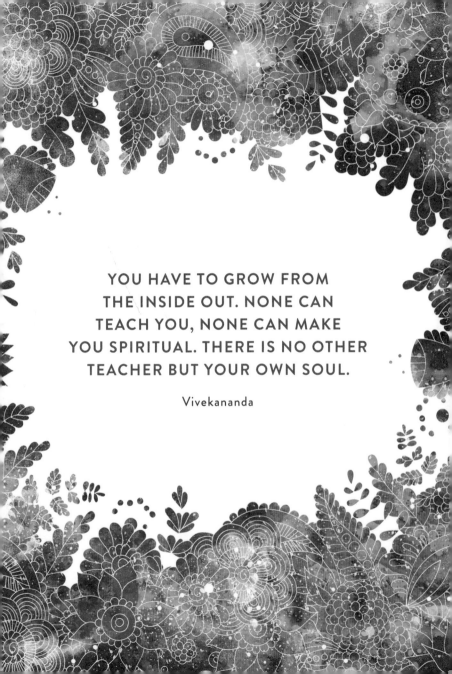

YOU HAVE TO GROW FROM
THE INSIDE OUT. NONE CAN
TEACH YOU, NONE CAN MAKE
YOU SPIRITUAL. THERE IS NO OTHER
TEACHER BUT YOUR OWN SOUL.

Vivekananda

QIGONG

Qigong is a system of movement and meditation that focuses on balancing the body's *chi*, or essential energy, to benefit body and mind. It has its roots in ancient Chinese culture and *qigong* translates as 'energy cultivation'. The system combines slow sequences of moves with breathing exercises and positive visualisations to explore the connection between mind, body and spirit.

Qigong is practised by millions of people the world over and many different forms have developed. Some are more dynamic – it can be used as martial arts training, for example – while others focus on static postures for healing particular ailments or meditative poses for spiritual development. (The health benefits of qigong are such that it is included on the syllabus of many medical schools in China.)

As there is such a variety of qigong styles, anyone can find a version to suit them, whatever their age or lifestyle. Whether you are seeking stress release, improved fitness or increased self-awareness, there's a form of qigong for you. The Internet is a great tool for finding out more, and there are numerous books, DVDs and classes available too.

Whatever style you choose, qigong allows you to reconnect with your spirit. At its heart are three simple principles: correct your posture, deepen your breathing and open your mind. If you aim to do these three things when you have a quiet moment, you'll be putting a little knowledge from this centuries-old system to good use.

DEVELOP A 'CAN DO' ATTITUDE

The most important lesson of qigong is that anyone can do it, so let go of any doubts you may feel about trying something new. Don't feel self-conscious or tell yourself that you won't be able to get it right. If you harbour these negative thoughts, you're giving in to the idea that you don't deserve nurturing or happiness. In order to find contentment, you must invest a little time and courage in seeking out a path.

EVERYTHING IS OUT
THERE WAITING FOR YOU. ALL
YOU HAVE TO DO IS WALK UP
AND DECLARE YOURSELF IN.

Stuart Wilde

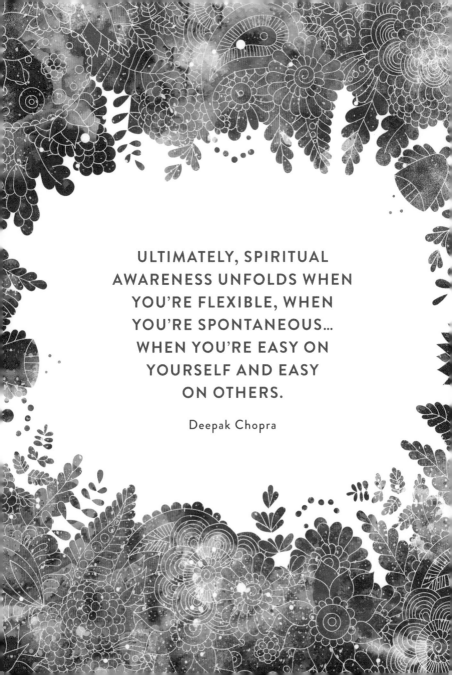

ULTIMATELY, SPIRITUAL AWARENESS UNFOLDS WHEN YOU'RE FLEXIBLE, WHEN YOU'RE SPONTANEOUS... WHEN YOU'RE EASY ON YOURSELF AND EASY ON OTHERS.

Deepak Chopra

START WITH A STRETCH

Stretching is something we usually do as part of a warm-up before we work out, but you can feel the benefits of a good stretch by making it a part of your everyday routine at home. On waking, stretch each part of your body in turn, starting from the toes and working upwards. Finish with a full body stretch. You'll release any tension in your muscles and start the day feeling calmer, more relaxed and ready for any challenge.

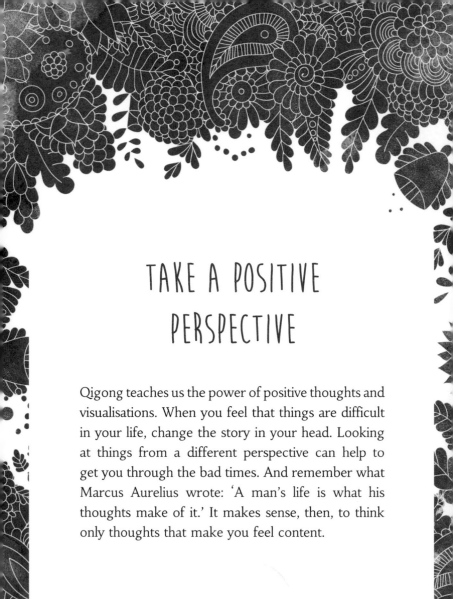

TAKE A POSITIVE PERSPECTIVE

Qigong teaches us the power of positive thoughts and visualisations. When you feel that things are difficult in your life, change the story in your head. Looking at things from a different perspective can help to get you through the bad times. And remember what Marcus Aurelius wrote: 'A man's life is what his thoughts make of it.' It makes sense, then, to think only thoughts that make you feel content.

STUDY ANIMAL FORMS

Many qigong poses are inspired by animals. These animal forms help us to focus on the different movements, qualities and energies of the creature in question, and develop them in ourselves. If you find yourself drawn to images of a particular animal, it may be worth exploring their symbolism and seeing if they have a message for you. Perhaps you need to develop the power of the tiger, the determination of the bear or the precision of the crane.

T'AI CHI

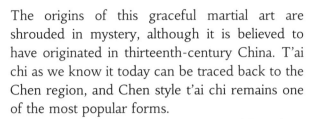

The origins of this graceful martial art are shrouded in mystery, although it is believed to have originated in thirteenth-century China. T'ai chi as we know it today can be traced back to the Chen region, and Chen style t'ai chi remains one of the most popular forms.

The practice combines solo routines with breathing and meditation exercises, alongside response drills and self-defence manoeuvres. There are several different schools of t'ai chi, some of which are more challenging than others. In addition, some classes blend characteristics of the different schools, but this diversity means that it's easy to find a class to suit you. T'ai chi is extremely popular and there is a wealth of information for the beginner to tap in to, both online and in the form of books, DVDs and courses.

The principle of yin and yang lies at the heart of this practice and is characterised in the t'ai chi symbol, which represents the balance of opposite forces in the universe and their continuous movement around a central point of stillness and calm. T'ai chi students learn to harness and balance their own energy, and to find clarity of mind while focusing on the flow of slow and deliberate movements. As with other holistic practices, it benefits students on a physical, emotional and spiritual level, and it has often been called meditation in motion.

LIFE IS MOVEMENT...
THE MORE FLUID
YOU ARE, THE MORE
YOU ARE ALIVE.

Arnaud Desjardins

EMBRACE CHANGE
AND MOVE FORWARD

There is always movement in life. When it is in chaos, find calm; when it is stagnant, move it along. Do not just sit and watch the world go by. You may not be able to control everything that happens to you, but you can control the way you react to life's ups and downs. Take responsibility for your situation and move forward with positivity.

TAKE A MEASURED APPROACH

In t'ai chi, students learn to use just enough strength to carry out each move – not too much and not too little – and so they achieve perfect balance. We can use this principle in many areas of our lives: in reacting appropriately to others, for instance. We can use enough strength to stand up for ourselves without being aggressive, but not too little or we become weak. We can learn to be firm but flexible, strong but loving.

HAPPINESS IS WHEN WHAT
YOU THINK, WHAT YOU SAY,
AND WHAT YOU DO
ARE IN HARMONY.

Mahatma Gandhi

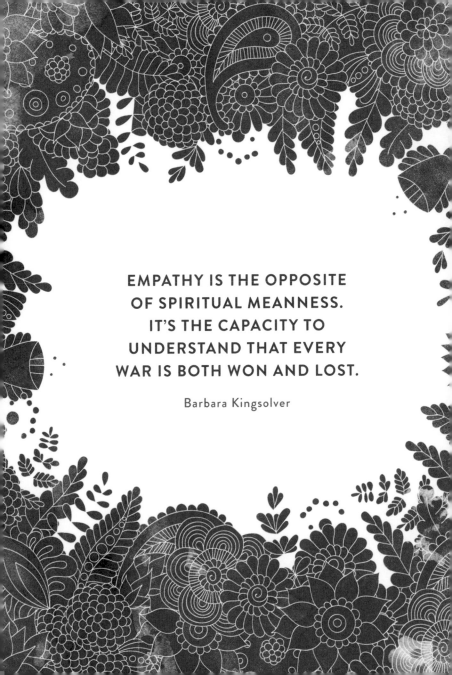

EMPATHY IS THE OPPOSITE
OF SPIRITUAL MEANNESS.
IT'S THE CAPACITY TO
UNDERSTAND THAT EVERY
WAR IS BOTH WON AND LOST.

Barbara Kingsolver

FIND UNITY IN DIVERSITY

The t'ai chi symbol reminds us that everything in creation is formed of a balance of opposites: we are all created the same and part of a greater whole. When you encounter challenging people, remind yourself that no one is essentially good or bad: we are all humans, doing our best to cope with life's twists and turns. You cannot know what turmoil others may be facing, so try to cultivate a loving and kind attitude to others – and to yourself.

AIKIDO

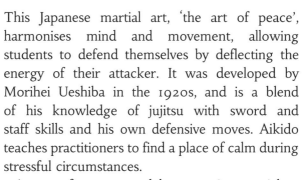

This Japanese martial art, 'the art of peace', harmonises mind and movement, allowing students to defend themselves by deflecting the energy of their attacker. It was developed by Morihei Ueshiba in the 1920s, and is a blend of his knowledge of jujitsu with sword and staff skills and his own defensive moves. Aikido teaches practitioners to find a place of calm during stressful circumstances.

A quest for peace and harmony is essential to the philosophy of aikido and this spiritual element was outlined in Ueshiba's writings. He explained that the correct mindset for a student is not to seek victory over their opponent, but to seek peace with the universe: 'True budo [martial arts practice] is the loving protection of all beings with a spirit of reconciliation.' Aikido moves typically involve either joint immobilisation or throws using the opponent's momentum.

Like t'ai chi, aikido is a popular activity and finding a local class should not be too challenging. As well as learning defensive skills, gaining confidence and improving your reflexes, aikido offers a spiritual dimension in which you can pursue inner peace and learn to take a step back from conflict. Aikido teaches us that meeting violence with violence is not the best way forward. It shows us the importance of acting rather than reacting and can help us to take control of the challenges we encounter in day-to-day life.

TRAIN YOUR REACTION REFLEX

Just as the student of aikido learns to hone their reflexes so that they react calmly and appropriately to whatever life throws at them, so we can learn to tune in to our intuition, trust our instinct and follow our inner spiritual guide. Remember: we cannot change the way other people behave, but we can control our response to them and train our reflexes so that we act in the most beneficial way.

PHYSICAL STRENGTH
CAN NEVER PERMANENTLY
WITHSTAND THE IMPACT
OF SPIRITUAL FORCE.

Franklin D. Roosevelt

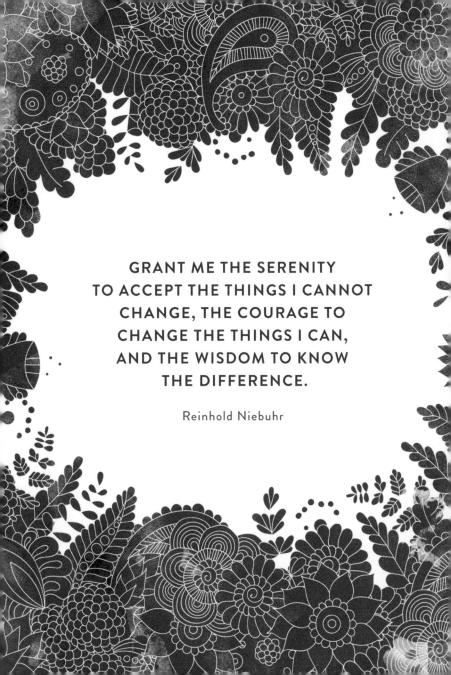

GRANT ME THE SERENITY
TO ACCEPT THE THINGS I CANNOT
CHANGE, THE COURAGE TO
CHANGE THE THINGS I CAN,
AND THE WISDOM TO KNOW
THE DIFFERENCE.

Reinhold Niebuhr

ABANDON ASSUMPTIONS

Morihei Ueshiba taught his students to stay calm under attack by releasing their attachment to life or death outcomes. We can become far too focused on achievements and expectations in the modern world. Put your faith in the spiritual and allow yourself to release your assumptions of how you feel your life should be. Learn to trust that the universe has your best interests at heart and cherish what you have, rather than longing for what you feel you deserve.

FASTING

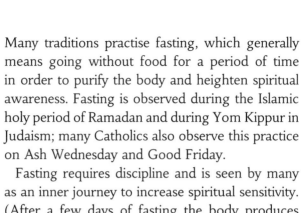

Many traditions practise fasting, which generally means going without food for a period of time in order to purify the body and heighten spiritual awareness. Fasting is observed during the Islamic holy period of Ramadan and during Yom Kippur in Judaism; many Catholics also observe this practice on Ash Wednesday and Good Friday.

Fasting requires discipline and is seen by many as an inner journey to increase spiritual sensitivity. (After a few days of fasting the body produces higher levels of endorphins, which increase alertness.) When the body and mind are not distracted by food, a person can better focus on nurturing their spirit instead of their body. Those who fast also learn to appreciate things that they normally take for granted.

There are many different approaches to fasting, some stricter than others. You may decide to limit your intake of anything but the plainest food for a short time or to rely on two simple meals a day for a longer period. Fasting will obviously have an effect on your body, and if you have any concerns about this, do check with your GP before trying it. Remember that your body will need to be hydrated and, if you are planning on fasting for more than a day or so, to have sufficient energy-giving foods or it will enter 'starvation mode' and start to break down muscle tissue rather than fat.

HAVE A SPIRITUAL DECLUTTER

'Healthy body, healthy mind' the saying goes, and this can extend to matters of the spirit, too. Just as improving our diet and replacing rich foods with simple unprocessed fare will benefit our physical health, so streamlining our thoughts – whether by fasting or meditation – will improve our state of mind and enhance our spirituality. Make an effort to declutter your life in this way and you'll notice that your soul soars.

REMEMBER HAPPINESS
DOESN'T DEPEND UPON WHO
YOU ARE OR WHAT YOU HAVE;
IT DEPENDS SOLELY ON
WHAT YOU THINK.

Dale Carnegie

THE MEANING OF LIFE
IS TO FIND YOUR GIFT.
THE PURPOSE OF LIFE
IS TO GIVE IT AWAY.

Pablo Picasso

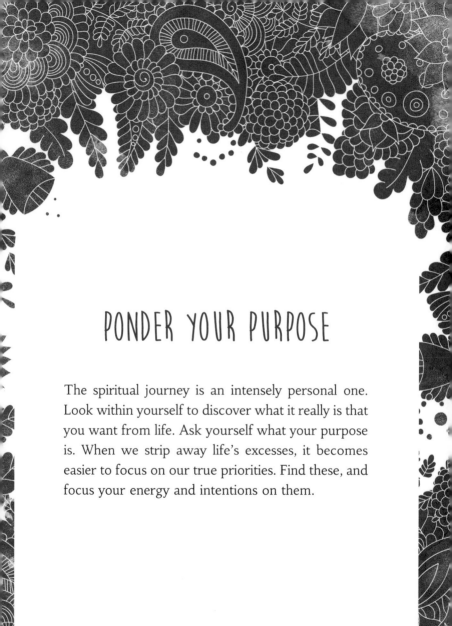

PONDER YOUR PURPOSE

The spiritual journey is an intensely personal one. Look within yourself to discover what it really is that you want from life. Ask yourself what your purpose is. When we strip away life's excesses, it becomes easier to focus on our true priorities. Find these, and focus your energy and intentions on them.

SOME PEOPLE GRUMBLE
THAT ROSES HAVE THORNS;
I AM GRATEFUL THAT
THORNS HAVE ROSES.

Jean-Baptiste Alphonse Karr

BE GRATEFUL

What makes you feel grateful in your life? Take time to think about these things and write them down. Consider what makes you feel better or happy – those things that give you a warm feeling inside. Practising gratitude will help you to focus on life's positive aspects. As you're drifting off to sleep at night, think back through your day and identify the one thing you're most grateful for. You'll go to sleep feeling happy and blessed.

CRYSTAL THERAPY

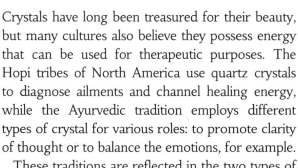

Crystals have long been treasured for their beauty, but many cultures also believe they possess energy that can be used for therapeutic purposes. The Hopi tribes of North America use quartz crystals to diagnose ailments and channel healing energy, while the Ayurvedic tradition employs different types of crystal for various roles: to promote clarity of thought or to balance the emotions, for example.

These traditions are reflected in the two types of crystal therapy available today. In the first method, a crystal (often quartz) is used to magnify the energy of a hands-on healer. In the second, crystals are placed around the person being treated or on their chakras (energy centres). There are seven major chakras in the body, and each is associated with a particular characteristic and colour. Crystals of a corresponding colour are used to balance the chakras' energies and promote healing.

Unlike traditional Western medicine, crystal therapy takes a holistic approach, treating the patient on a spiritual and emotional level alongside their physical symptoms. Seek out a crystal therapist via the Federation of Holistic Therapists (see Further Information) or tap in to the healing qualities of crystals in your everyday life by using them around the home: a piece of quartz on your desk to counter the effects of the electromagnetic field of your computer, for example. Although crystals can be bought online, it is a good idea to handle them before you buy, as you may well be drawn by a particular crystal's energy.

TUNE IN TO A CRYSTAL

Experience the energy of crystals by visiting a crystal shop and letting your intuition help you when choosing one (or more) to take home. You can hold your crystal while meditating, keep it by your bedside or carry it with you every day. Look up its properties and you're sure to find that they will resonate with you on a physical, emotional or spiritual level.

EVERY PARTICULAR IN
NATURE, A LEAF, A DROP,
A CRYSTAL, A MOMENT OF TIME
IS RELATED TO THE WHOLE,
AND PARTAKES OF THE
PERFECTION OF THE WHOLE.

Ralph Waldo Emerson

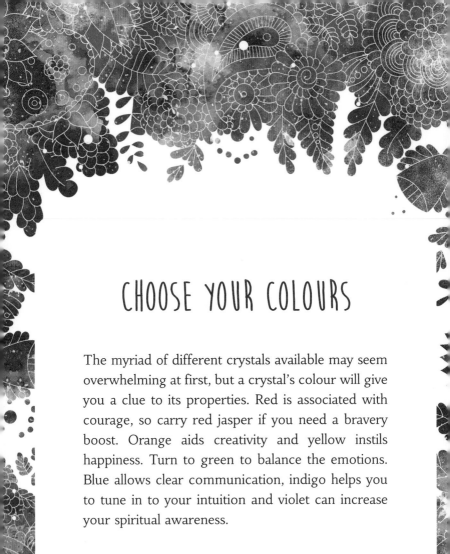

CHOOSE YOUR COLOURS

The myriad of different crystals available may seem overwhelming at first, but a crystal's colour will give you a clue to its properties. Red is associated with courage, so carry red jasper if you need a bravery boost. Orange aids creativity and yellow instils happiness. Turn to green to balance the emotions. Blue allows clear communication, indigo helps you to tune in to your intuition and violet can increase your spiritual awareness.

LOCATE YOUR CHAKRAS

For more powerful healing, use a crystal in conjunction with the relevant chakra point in your body.

Chakra	Location	Colour
Root	Base of spine	Red
Sacral	Just below navel	Orange
Solar plexus	Base of ribcage	Yellow
Heart	Centre of chest	Green
Throat	Base of throat	Blue
Third eye	Above and between brows	Indigo
Crown	Top of head	Violet

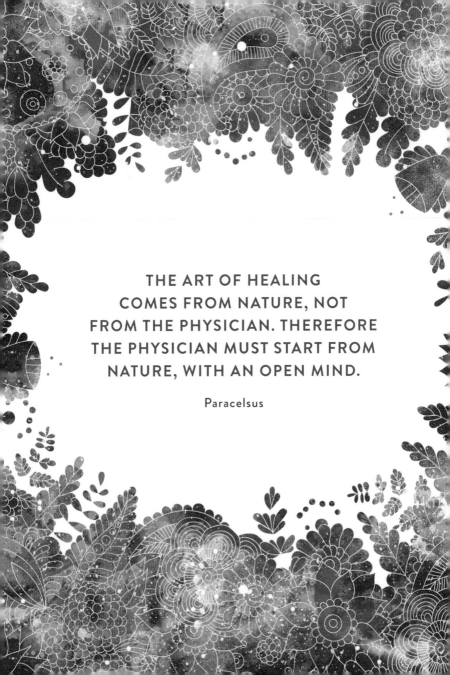

THE ART OF HEALING
COMES FROM NATURE, NOT
FROM THE PHYSICIAN. THEREFORE
THE PHYSICIAN MUST START FROM
NATURE, WITH AN OPEN MIND.

Paracelsus

TRY A CRYSTAL MEDITATION

If you are experiencing a particular imbalance or problem, look up the relevant crystal/chakra to focus on (or use one for each chakra and perform a general balancing meditation). Lie down comfortably and place your crystal over or next to the corresponding chakra. Take some slow breaths and then visualise coloured healing energy emanating from the crystal and flowing through your body. (Work from the root chakra up if you are balancing all the chakras.)

REIKI

Reiki – which means 'universal life energy' in Japanese – is a treatment in which the practitioner channels healing energy through the recipient. Like many holistic practices, it is based on the manipulation of the life energy that flows through all of us (known in Japanese as *ki*). By placing their hands over various points in the body (including the seven main chakras – see Crystal Therapy), a reiki therapist is able to identify any energy blockages, and rebalance and realign energy flow throughout the body.

Reiki was developed by a Buddhist, Mikao Usui, in the 1920s. Usui went on to add a spiritual element to the practice when he outlined his Five Reiki Ideals: do not anger; do not worry; be filled with gratitude; devote yourself to your work; and be kind to others. He felt that it was important for reiki recipients to take responsibility for their own spiritual healing by resolving to improve themselves in this way.

Reiki is a relaxing, non-intrusive treatment. Some people feel sensations of tingling or heat during a session. They may experience an emotional reaction too, as the chakras are rebalanced. The best way to benefit from reiki is to try a taster session (these are often available at holistic fairs) or check online to find a therapist. You can also be taught to practise reiki yourself – a weekend course is enough to get you started at a basic level, allowing self-treatment.

REMOVE NEGATIVITY

When we think negative thoughts, we can start to see ourselves in a damaging way. Reiki teaches us that taking negativity on board can be detrimental to our life energy, disrupting its flow. Usui taught his students to focus on positives and fill their lives with gratitude. Embrace happiness by letting go of negative beliefs and emotions; these are holding you back in life.

IT IS THE UNSEEN
AND THE SPIRITUAL
IN PEOPLE THAT
DETERMINES THE
OUTWARD AND
THE ACTUAL.

Oswald Chambers

REIKI IS LOVE,
LOVE IS WHOLENESS,
WHOLENESS IS BALANCE,
BALANCE IS WELL BEING,
WELL BEING IS FREEDOM
FROM DISEASE.

Mikao Usui

TAKE CONTROL OF YOUR SPIRITUAL DEVELOPMENT

In a reiki treatment we benefit from our therapist's work, but we must take responsibility for our own self-development, too, making a conscious effort to improve ourselves as human beings. Learn to live more spiritually by aiming to grow in openness, prudence and wisdom. Although this may push your boundaries in new directions, you will soon feel the benefits.

MODERN PAGANISM

Paganism in general refers to the religious traditions of a country's indigenous population and is an umbrella term for many ancient spiritual beliefs, but here in the West paganism refers to a more specific spiritual path. Modern pagans, such as Druids or Wiccans, share a deep reverence for nature, and an understanding that all life is connected and should be respected. (Many choose to follow an eco-friendly lifestyle.)

Modern pagans observe the cycle of the seasons, the moon and life itself (from birth to death), and eight annual festivals are celebrated throughout the year. These mark the 'turn of the wheel' and tie in to the natural cycles of the planet. They include the equinoxes, solstices and four additional seasonal festivals. Pagans feel that our lives can be lived in harmony with these changes; for example, that it is beneficial to plan new projects in the spring.

For pagans, connecting with nature is an important part of their spiritual practice in a world where many of us feel that we've lost that natural connection. We spend our time in centrally heated buildings and tend to follow the same daily routine week in, week out. Studies have shown the benefits of spending time in nature, so incorporating elements of a pagan outlook into our lives can have a huge positive impact on our mental and physical well-being.

TAP IN TO TREE ENERGY

Spend time in nature and you will feel uplifted. Trees give off positive energy and walking among them not only alleviates stress, but also boosts the immune system. Pagans believe that different trees embody different characteristics: so if you need an extra boost of strength, sit beneath an oak tree; get some perspective on things by seeking out a fir tree or balance your emotions in the company of a willow.

I GO TO NATURE TO BE
SOOTHED AND HEALED,
AND TO HAVE MY
SENSES PUT IN ORDER.

John Burroughs

ENGAGE WITH THE ELEMENTS

Pagans use the different elements – earth, water, air and fire – to enhance various characteristics in their lives. If you feel unsettled, try grounding yourself by walking barefoot on the grass or sand. To release pent-up emotions, soak in a warm bath or spend time near water. Sharpen your thinking by getting out and about on a blustery day and breathing in the fresh air. Use candlelight and fire to help your intuition and passions to burn more brightly.

MIRROR THE SEASONS

Connect with the cycle of the seasons by making a fresh start in the spring and sowing the seeds of new projects for the year ahead. Soak in the warmth of the sun's rays in the summer and re-energise. At harvest time, give thanks for the good things in your life. And as the trees lose their leaves in winter, take stock of your life and shed any possessions or habits that are no longer useful to you.

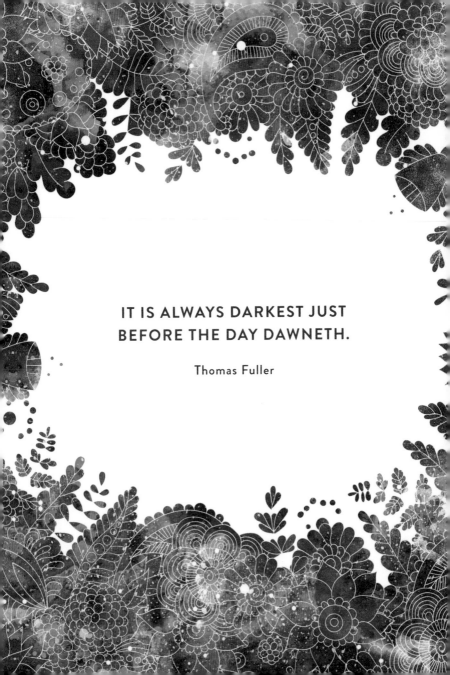

IT IS ALWAYS DARKEST JUST
BEFORE THE DAY DAWNETH.

Thomas Fuller

THE TURN OF THE WHEEL

Paganism recognises the cyclical nature of life: out of every ending comes a new beginning. In order to move forward, we have to learn to let go of the past. The world is ever changing, the wheel ever turning – just as dawn follows the darkest hour of night, happier times follow on from those of trial and difficulty. Learn to be patient and remember: dark times will pass and make way for bright, new beginnings.

SHAMANISM

Shamanism is often associated with Native American culture, but shamanic practices have existed in indigenous populations the world over for centuries. They all have one key belief at their core: everything in nature has a spirit and wisdom to share. Shamanism involves tapping in to this universal wisdom – often through 'journeying' – to heal individuals at a spiritual level. During journeying the shamanic healer will use drumming or singing to enter an altered state and access an otherworldly dimension where they can receive wisdom from past ancestors or animal guides.

Shamanic healing can also involve 'soul retrieval'. Practitioners believe that when we experience shocking events, we lose fragments of our soul, or we may give fragments away during intense relationships. Journeying allows a healer to help a person to retrieve these fragments and recover from past traumas.

As it is based in the ancient cultures of indigenous people, shamanic wisdom helps us to connect with our ancestors when we include it in our everyday lives. Its basic principles are to embrace nature, to heal the environment, others and oneself, and to set aside time to journey (or meditate) regularly and work on unifying the mind, body and spirit. Many shamanic teachers offer introductory workshops where people can discover more about shamanism and even learn to journey.

RELAXING RHYTHMS

Shamanic healers often use drums or rattles to enter the meditative state needed for journeying. Listening to a repeated tempo of between four and seven beats per second will cause the brain to enter a theta-wave state. (We all experience this during light sleep and many people achieve it during deep meditation.) If you find meditating a challenge, it could be worth listening to shamanic drumming online – or even investing in your own drum or rattle – to help you.

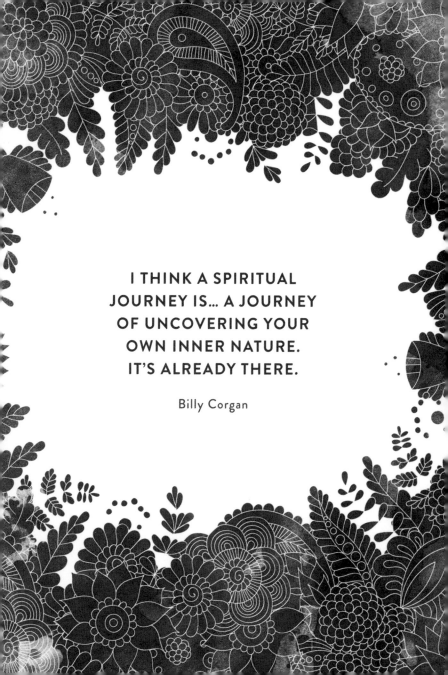

I THINK A SPIRITUAL
JOURNEY IS... A JOURNEY
OF UNCOVERING YOUR
OWN INNER NATURE.
IT'S ALREADY THERE.

Billy Corgan

HEAL WITH HERBS

Plant herbs in a pot to keep around the house or in the garden. Fresh herbs bring you into direct contact with nature, which is the first step to finding physical and spiritual balance. Herbs are well known for their medicinal uses too: check reputable resources online or find a book on herbal remedies by an acknowledged expert and you'll have access to centuries-old wisdom on treating virtually any ailment.

MAKE A PILGRIMAGE

An important aspect of shamanism involves honouring natural wonders and showing reverence for places that are important to us. Make a pilgrimage to somewhere that calls to you: it may be somewhere new that you've longed to visit, a place from your past or somewhere that had significance for your ancestors. Make time to appreciate your surroundings while you are there. You're sure to come away with an enlightened sense of self and a renewed appreciation of the world around you.

WE ARE ALL
VISIONARIES
AND WHAT WE SEE
IS OUR SOUL
IN THINGS.

Henri-Frédéric
Amiel

SEEING YOUR SPIRIT ANIMAL

Shamans work with animal guides and believe that all of us have power animals beside us in a spiritual form. We attract different guides at different stages of our life, so your spirit animal may change. Pay attention to any creatures that crop up in dreams or that you find yourself drawn to in books, as well as trying an animal meditation or using oracle cards, to discover your companion and their symbolism or relevance to you.

SPIRITUAL
HEALING

Many religious movements have a tradition of spiritual healing, although today's practitioners are often not followers of a particular faith. There are various forms of spiritual healing, but all involve the practitioner drawing on universal energy for beneficial results. This may be done through meditation, prayer or hands-on therapy in a manner similar to reiki.

Spiritual healers are able to detect a person's aura – the multi-layered energy field that surrounds each of us. (If you've ever picked up 'vibes' from someone else, you were tuning in to their aura.) Healers are highly sensitive to these energy messages and are able to learn a lot about a person's past, present and future by reading their aura. They can then go on to discuss any issues as well as directing healing energy to where it is needed.

Spiritual healing is the most widely practised alternative therapy, and it has irrefutable positive results. (The NHS employs healers to help seriously ill patients.) The most important lesson we can learn from it is about the power of kind thoughts and intentions. Focusing our goodwill and positivity on another individual (or ourselves) can have a huge beneficial impact. Practise every day and see the results of your compassion.

FOR ATTRACTIVE
LIPS, SPEAK WORDS
OF KINDNESS. FOR
LOVELY EYES, SEEK OUT
THE GOOD IN PEOPLE.

Sam Levenson

SEND HEALING ENERGY

We are all familiar with the feeling of comfort that a hug can bring, but we can learn to project feelings of positivity to our loved ones across the miles, too. Spiritual energy is not limited by geography so try sending healing vibes to someone you know who needs them. Sit quietly and think about your chosen person. Consider what you admire about them, then think about what they might need – love, courage, comfort or peace – and send them those thoughts.

TUNE IN TO VIBES

We can all learn to be more sensitive to people's vibes and use this sensitivity to enhance our relationships. Take a moment to see what you can detect about someone's energy: are they in a good mood or feeling harassed? Are they in need of comfort? And how does *your* energy change when you are with them? Do you feel boosted or wary? Your physical reaction is more telling than your mind's, so tune in to that.

FRIENDSHIP HAS ALWAYS BELONGED TO THE CORE OF MY SPIRITUAL JOURNEY.

Henri Nouwen

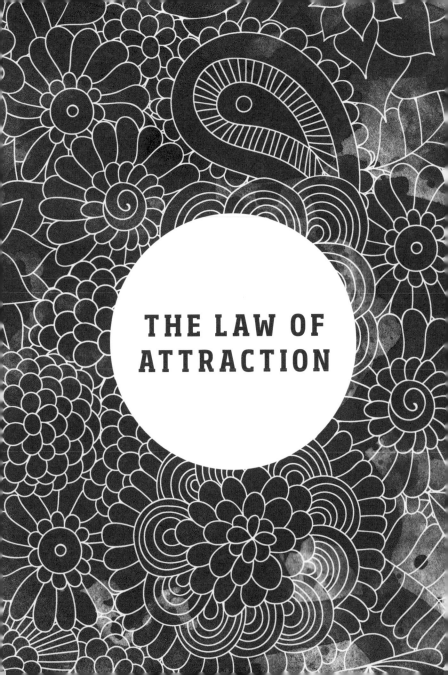

THE LAW OF ATTRACTION

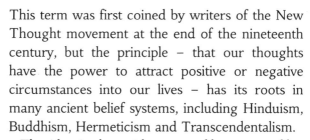

This term was first coined by writers of the New Thought movement at the end of the nineteenth century, but the principle – that our thoughts have the power to attract positive or negative circumstances into our lives – has its roots in many ancient belief systems, including Hinduism, Buddhism, Hermeticism and Transcendentalism.

The idea is that with energy, like attracts like: things that vibrate at the same frequency are drawn to one another. If we focus predominantly on our fears that a specific negative event will come to pass, for example, we are more likely to find ourselves in that situation than if we focus on a positive outcome. The Law of Attraction teaches us to use the power of positive thinking and visualisation to change our lives for the better.

Scientific studies into the effects of an optimistic attitude show overwhelmingly positive results. The benefits it can have on our lives include higher levels of achievement, improved health and a better ability to recover from stressful events. Even the most pessimistic of us can learn to practise positivity. The Law of Attraction is a hot topic and there is a plethora of books available to get you started on a more positive path, but you can see immediate results just by making a few simple changes to your daily life.

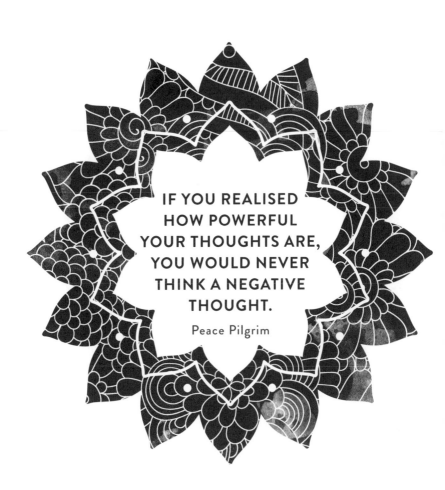

IF YOU REALISED
HOW POWERFUL
YOUR THOUGHTS ARE,
YOU WOULD NEVER
THINK A NEGATIVE
THOUGHT.

Peace Pilgrim

SAY NO TO NEGATIVITY

Replace negativity with positivity in all aspects of your life. When you're talking about future plans, do you find yourself saying things like: 'It'll probably never work but...'? Replace these negative phrases with positive ones, and you'll bring more energy and enthusiasm to each new challenge you face. And don't allow other people's negative opinions to bring you down. You are the one who ultimately decides whether or not you will reach your goals – nobody else!

ATTRACT
HAPPINESS

If you want to feel happier, attract some joy into your life by including more laughter in your day. (When we laugh, we cannot help but feel better, as laughter releases endorphins into our bloodstream.) You know what works best for you: whether it's having a chat with your funniest friend or watching an episode of your favourite sitcom.

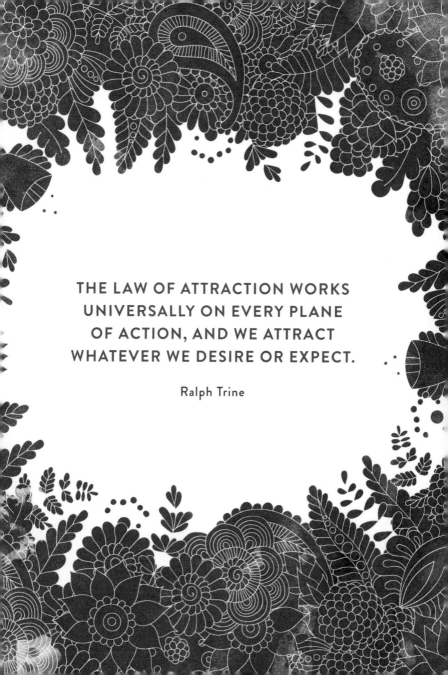

THE LAW OF ATTRACTION WORKS
UNIVERSALLY ON EVERY PLANE
OF ACTION, AND WE ATTRACT
WHATEVER WE DESIRE OR EXPECT.

Ralph Trine

KARMA

The idea that our every action has consequences (either in this life or the next) is familiar to us through expressions such as 'You reap what you sow'. Karma is central to many ancient belief systems. Buddhism, Hinduism, Sikhism and Jainism all emphasise the importance of the karmic principle: good deeds will lead to happy consequences; bad deeds will cause us future suffering.

Many religions are built around the belief that the soul moves on to a new body after death – and so the sins of past lives may be carried forward to result in negative experiences in the present (and future). They believe that past lives can affect the family a person is surrounded by, as well as their self-belief and even their health.

Whether you believe in reincarnation or not, it's certainly the case that a person who does good deeds is more likely to trigger a positive reaction in others than a person who does not. Scientific studies prove that showing compassion affects the hormones that are released into our bloodstream: thoughts of kindness produce oxytocin, which makes us more trusting, less anxious and more receptive to others' emotions. By actively choosing to behave in a kind manner, we will feel happier and be better equipped to build strong relationships. Repeatedly behaving in this way will change our neural pathways, too, and make us more likely to repeat that type of behaviour in the future.

THREE THINGS IN
HUMAN LIFE ARE IMPORTANT:
THE FIRST IS TO BE KIND;
THE SECOND IS TO BE KIND;
AND THE THIRD IS TO BE KIND.

Henry James

SEE THE CONSEQUENCES OF KINDNESS

Practise kindness whenever you can and you will soon see the consequences. You could, for example, donate to or volunteer for a charity you believe is worthwhile. Whether you are giving your money or your time, being more generous in your actions will benefit you as well as those you help. Learn to give selflessly and you will gain a stronger sense of purpose in your life.

DON'T WASTE YOUR WORDS

It's all too easy to get drawn in to listening to unpleasant talk about others, but words – like actions – have consequences, and lending your ear to this sort of negativity can only be a bad thing. Words are a wonderful tool for spreading joy and happiness so avoid wasting them. Choose to pay someone a compliment instead. You'll both feel the benefits.

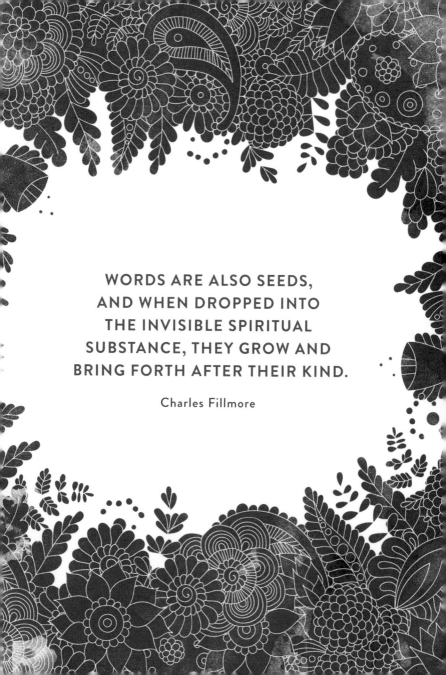

WORDS ARE ALSO SEEDS,
AND WHEN DROPPED INTO
THE INVISIBLE SPIRITUAL
SUBSTANCE, THEY GROW AND
BRING FORTH AFTER THEIR KIND.

Charles Fillmore

A MAN IS BUT
THE PRODUCT OF
HIS THOUGHTS.
WHAT HE THINKS,
HE BECOMES.

Mahatma Gandhi

CONSIDER THE CONSEQUENCES

The principle of karma reminds us that every choice we make will have consequences. Be mindful of this every day and take the time to consider your actions carefully. What are the possible consequences of your decision? Taking responsibility for your life in this way can help you to overcome 'victimhood' and take control of your destiny.

THEOSOPHY

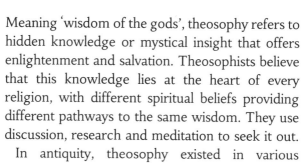

Meaning 'wisdom of the gods', theosophy refers to hidden knowledge or mystical insight that offers enlightenment and salvation. Theosophists believe that this knowledge lies at the heart of every religion, with different spiritual beliefs providing different pathways to the same wisdom. They use discussion, research and meditation to seek it out.

In antiquity, theosophy existed in various forms, but the modern movement was set up in the United States in the late nineteenth century. Individuals decide on their own principles to live by, which often reflect the beliefs at the heart of the movement: that all life is one entity (so by helping others we are helping ourselves); that life and death are part of a continuous cycle; and that the purpose of life is to learn. Theosophists respect nature and the environment, and may choose to be vegetarian. They often actively support human rights movements and strive for all forms of equality.

As theosophy draws together all religions (along with science and philosophy), it regards humanity as part of a single spiritual family and teaches us to approach others with compassion and understanding, even when their views may seem very different from our own.

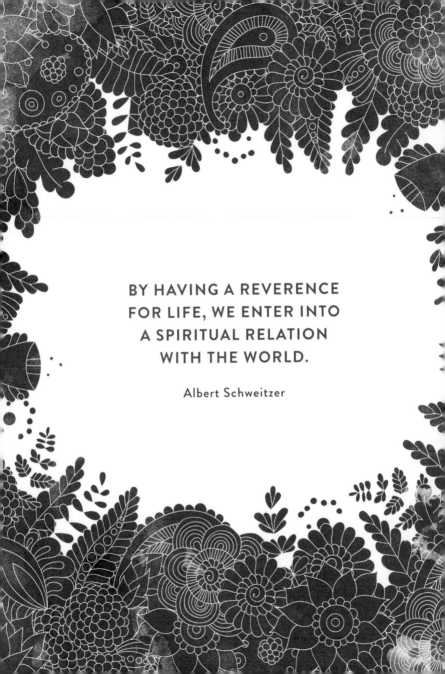

BY HAVING A REVERENCE
FOR LIFE, WE ENTER INTO
A SPIRITUAL RELATION
WITH THE WORLD.

Albert Schweitzer

READ A SPIRITUAL BOOK

Thinking about spirituality might not be something we do regularly, and might even feel uncomfortable, but we shouldn't let that put us off trying to connect with something fundamental that is within all of us. To get you thinking about spiritual matters, explore the Mind, Body and Spirit section of your local bookshop and see if a title jumps out at you. Whether you agree with what you read or not, it will be a good starting point.

WRITE DOWN
YOUR PRINCIPLES

The spiritual journey is an intensely personal one, and everyone will have a different experience. Look within yourself to discover your beliefs and then take some time to consider what is really important to you. You may want to list your priorities: the principles by which you would like to live your life and the things you would like to be remembered for. This will give you a sense of direction and help you to discover your true purpose.

DISCOVER OTHER PATHS

Take time to learn about other types of belief systems. Develop an open mind in order to discover ideas and points of view different from your own. Talk to friends about their beliefs and pay attention to the different views of those around you. Attending community events can be a great way of meeting people from different faiths and learning about their spiritual pathway.

SEEK SIMILARITIES

A good way to defuse an argument is to seek out similarities with the person confronting you. It's all too easy to focus on your differences at difficult times, but finding common ground can pave the way forward. Remember that how you feel about others' characteristics often has much to reveal about your own traits. If you pick up on someone's tendency to boast, for example, take an honest look at your behaviour. Is this something that you do too?

EVERYTHING THAT
IRRITATES US ABOUT
OTHERS CAN LEAD US
TO AN UNDERSTANDING
OF OURSELVES.

Carl Jung

HINDUISM

Often regarded as the world's oldest religion, Hinduism is actually an umbrella term for a collection of spiritual, philosophical and cultural ideas characterised by the law of karma and the idea of the immortality of the soul. Hinduism has its roots in the Vedic traditions that developed in India over three thousand years ago. With its long history, Hinduism has absorbed many religious beliefs over time and tolerance is an important part of its approach.

Three deities are central to Hinduism: Brahma (the supreme creator), Vishnu (the preserver) and Shiva (the destroyer). In addition to these, Hindus are free to choose which deities they worship, and many local gods and goddesses may be acknowledged in their daily rituals. (Yoga is often used as a way to still the mind and gain spiritual insight.)

Broadly, Hinduism outlines four goals in life: to live by an agreed moral code, to lawfully pursue material gain, to understand and respect the concept of karma, and – ultimately – to aim for the soul to be released from the constant cycle of rebirth (to achieve *moksha*). An individual can do this through a life of hard work, selfless actions and devotion to their chosen deities.

Another important aspect of contemporary Hinduism is the pursuit of justice through non-violent means, as extolled by Mahatma Gandhi. His philosophy of non-violence encourages us to love all and hate no one.

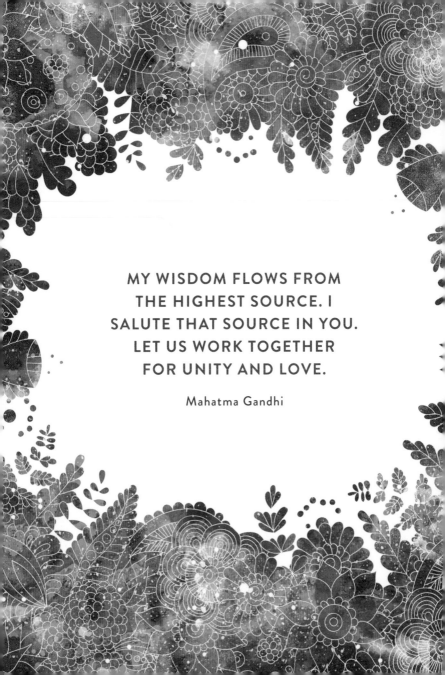

MY WISDOM FLOWS FROM
THE HIGHEST SOURCE. I
SALUTE THAT SOURCE IN YOU.
LET US WORK TOGETHER
FOR UNITY AND LOVE.

Mahatma Gandhi

MAKE TIME FOR A MEETING

As a philosophy, Hinduism invites us to examine our relationship with the divine, our relationships with one another and our relationship with ourselves. Hindus are expected to devote a little time every day to this spiritual work. Why not try praying or meditating regularly, alone or in a group? You may find that attending a weekly meditation meeting will help you to make spiritual contemplation a regular part of your life.

WORK HARD TO
REAP REWARDS

Your inner potential has no limits. It is up to you to decide how much you want to make of it. We can so easily drift from day to day, feeling that we are a victim of life's circumstances, but remember that you are at the helm of your ship. Take responsibility, plot your course and steer your life in whichever direction you choose. No one, except yourself, is holding you back from anything.

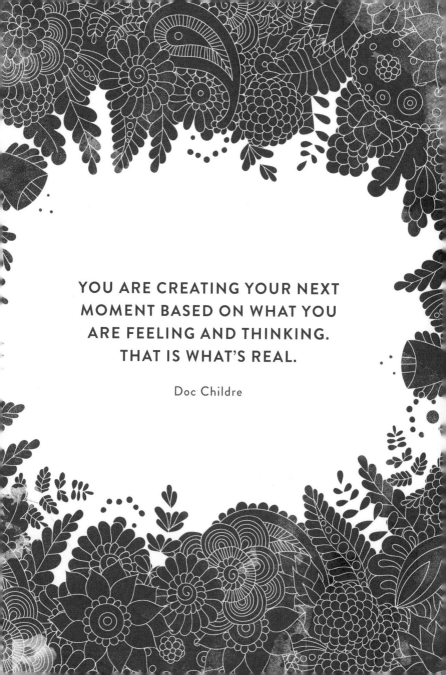

YOU ARE CREATING YOUR NEXT
MOMENT BASED ON WHAT YOU
ARE FEELING AND THINKING.
THAT IS WHAT'S REAL.

Doc Childre

BUDDHISM

Buddhists pursue the spiritual state of enlightenment through practices such as meditation, reflection and rituals. They follow the path of the Buddha, Siddhartha Gautama, who began his own quest for enlightenment between the sixth and fifth centuries BCE. Buddhism can be seen as a philosophy rather than a religion, as Buddhists do not worship deities. (Indeed, Gautama's teachings were the result of his years of life experience and contemplation, and not the received wisdom of a prophet.)

Unlike religions such as Hinduism that see the soul as eternal, Buddhism suggests that nothing is fixed, and change is always possible. It asserts that human suffering is caused by our belief that things can last and our craving for things to be a certain way. Only when we let go of such cravings can we truly be happy. Buddhism's Noble Eightfold Path outlines how we can achieve this by cultivating wisdom, virtue and mindfulness.

In practical terms Buddhism is a flexible belief system that may be applied easily to everyday life. Although it is an ancient philosophy, in a modern world where speed, achievement and conspicuous consumption are highly prized, it has much to offer. Buddhists are known for their peaceful demeanour, charity and compassion towards others.

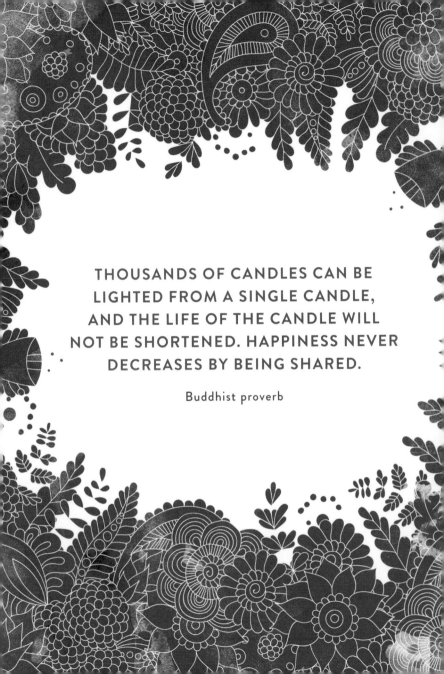

THOUSANDS OF CANDLES CAN BE
LIGHTED FROM A SINGLE CANDLE,
AND THE LIFE OF THE CANDLE WILL
NOT BE SHORTENED. HAPPINESS NEVER
DECREASES BY BEING SHARED.

Buddhist proverb

GIVE SOMETHING BACK

Charitable endeavour, like faith, gives meaning to our lives and is a truly reliable source of joy. There are so many ways you can give something back to your community. You're bound to be able to find something that appeals to you, whether it's working for a wildlife charity, helping at a youth group or taking time to chat to someone who is housebound. Visit www.do-it.org to find dozens of opportunities to help others near you.

FIND THE MIDDLE WAY

The Buddha taught that neither a life of luxury nor one of austerity would aid spiritual development and bring happiness. He recommended following a balanced lifestyle – the Middle Way – in which individuals develop the discipline to live an ethical life. A balanced approach can be beneficial in many areas of our lives, so strive to cultivate discipline and avoid over-indulging, but do not deny yourself life's pleasures either.

DON'T DWELL ON PAINFUL EXPERIENCES

We all encounter difficult situations in life. The pain of the experience itself is upsetting enough, but many of us tend to relive upsetting moments time and again, prolonging our discomfort, in a reaction that Buddhists call the second arrow of suffering. Remember that while we may be unable to control what happens in life, we can control our thoughts. Resolve not to dwell on difficult situations and avoid the pain of the second arrow.

ANGER BEGETS
MORE ANGER, AND
FORGIVENESS AND
LOVE LEAD TO MORE
FORGIVENESS
AND LOVE.

Mahavira

NURTURE
UNCONDITIONAL LOVE

When you follow your spiritual path, try to tune in to a feeling of unconditional love for others and yourself. Change negative aspects into positive ones, even when you need to summon up inner strength to do this. You may find that meditating or practising mindfulness will help you to detach from any negative reactions that you are experiencing. Cultivate a feeling of loving kindness and acceptance instead, and remember to draw on this in challenging times.

JAINISM

This ancient Indian belief system was shaped into its present form by Mahavira, a religious reformer born in 599 BCE, whom Jains believe to be the latest in a line of spiritual teachers. There are no gods in Jainism; the goal of spiritual life is to achieve release from the cycle of reincarnation by freeing the soul from all karma (good or bad). Full responsibility for achieving this falls on individuals and how they conduct themselves.

Followers strive to live a life of self-denial and achieve five key principles: chastity, no lying, no stealing, non-attachment and non-violence. The latter is most important and – as Jains believe that all living things have souls – it extends to all creatures, not just fellow human beings. Followers are strict vegetarians and choose to live in the most eco-friendly way possible.

Meditation is an important part of daily spiritual practice and Jains follow the Path of the Three Jewels in order to embody the key principles of their religion. These jewels are: right conduct, right faith and right knowledge. Atonement for sins is another key principle; individuals must confess their sins from the past year to family and friends at the annual Paryushana festival, when all pledge to move forward without bearing grudges.

CLEAR THE AIR

Our relationships will never reach their true potential if we are weighed down by past disagreements or misunderstandings. If a relationship is worth nurturing, make the effort to clear the air, talk through any unresolved issues and agree to leave these in the past. Move forward, free of grudges and resentment, and enjoy the positive energy of a refreshed relationship lived fully in the present moment.

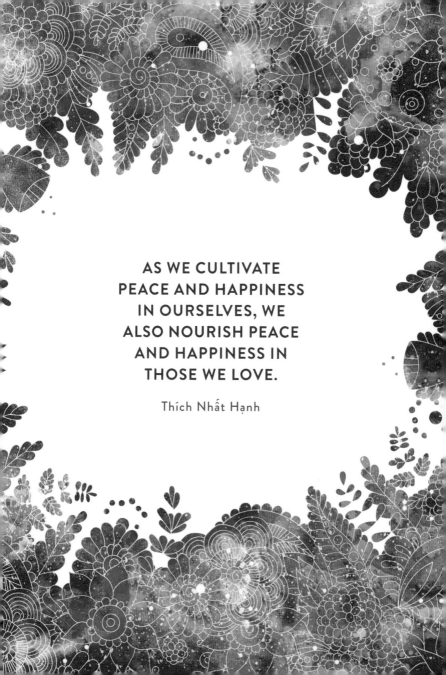

AS WE CULTIVATE
PEACE AND HAPPINESS
IN OURSELVES, WE
ALSO NOURISH PEACE
AND HAPPINESS IN
THOSE WE LOVE.

Thích Nhất Hạnh

WE HAVE FORGOTTEN
HOW TO BE GOOD GUESTS,
HOW TO WALK LIGHTLY ON
THE EARTH AS ITS OTHER
CREATURES DO.

Barbara Ward

MAKE ECO-FRIENDLY CHOICES

Jainism teaches us to consider the impact of our lives on other living creatures and the world around us. While vegetarianism may not be for you, you might decide to look into where the food you buy is sourced and make different choices accordingly. Are there other ways in which you could soften your impact on the planet? When we consider our relationship with other living things, we learn to value all life more, including our own.

CONFUCIANISM

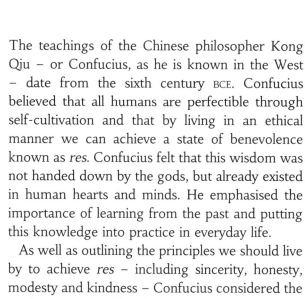

The teachings of the Chinese philosopher Kong Qiu – or Confucius, as he is known in the West – date from the sixth century BCE. Confucius believed that all humans are perfectible through self-cultivation and that by living in an ethical manner we can achieve a state of benevolence known as *res*. Confucius felt that this wisdom was not handed down by the gods, but already existed in human hearts and minds. He emphasised the importance of learning from the past and putting this knowledge into practice in everyday life.

As well as outlining the principles we should live by to achieve *res* – including sincerity, honesty, modesty and kindness – Confucius considered the qualities we should cultivate in our relationships with others, as parents, children, siblings and friends, for example. He gave great weight to the importance of embracing our roles in life and carrying them out in the appropriate manner.

Though not overtly spiritual with regard to focusing on the elusive or ethereal, Confucianism asserts that by achieving *res* and enacting this in our everyday lives, we can forge a stronger connection with our spiritual side and realise our full potential.

LEARN TO LIVE BETTER

There are no such things as mistakes. Even when we feel we have taken a wrong turn in life and perhaps gone on to regret our actions, we can find something of value in what has happened. What have you learned about yourself and how you behave in certain situations? How could you handle things differently in future? Regard everything in life as a lesson and you will become wiser in the art of living.

OUR GREATEST
GLORY IS NOT IN
NEVER FALLING,
BUT IN RISING
EVERY TIME WE FALL.

Confucius

CULTIVATE *RES*

The five constant virtues of Confucianism, which we should strive to uphold in our everyday behaviour, are: honesty, modesty, kindness, diligence and sincerity. Together these qualities embody *res* ('goodness'). Consider what these qualities mean to you. When was the last time you experienced these attributes in others? Do you embody these virtues in your day-to-day life or is there, perhaps, one that you could try to cultivate more often?

FOCUS ON RELATIONSHIPS

Confucius outlined the qualities we should bring to the roles we play in life – such as being a dutiful child or a considerate friend. In the modern world our interactions with others may be rushed, so taking time to focus on our relationships is hugely beneficial. Concentrate on radiating acceptance when you interact with someone dear to you; listen to them mindfully (with all your attention) and you will improve your relationship instantly.

TO BE WRONGED
IS NOTHING UNLESS
YOU CONTINUE TO
REMEMBER IT.

Confucius

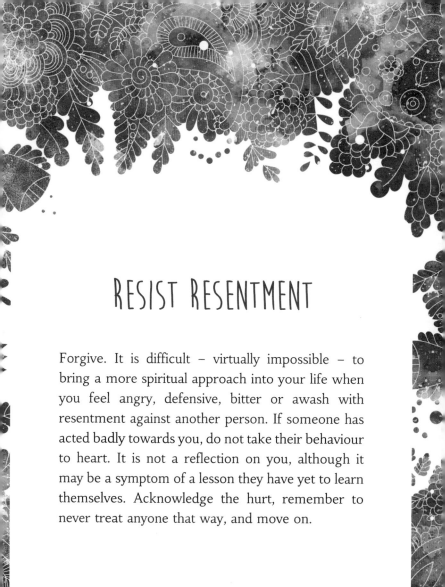

Resist Resentment

Forgive. It is difficult – virtually impossible – to bring a more spiritual approach into your life when you feel angry, defensive, bitter or awash with resentment against another person. If someone has acted badly towards you, do not take their behaviour to heart. It is not a reflection on you, although it may be a symptom of a lesson they have yet to learn themselves. Acknowledge the hurt, remember to never treat anyone that way, and move on.

SHINTO

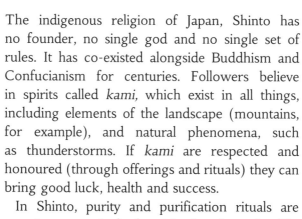

The indigenous religion of Japan, Shinto has no founder, no single god and no single set of rules. It has co-existed alongside Buddhism and Confucianism for centuries. Followers believe in spirits called *kami,* which exist in all things, including elements of the landscape (mountains, for example), and natural phenomena, such as thunderstorms. If *kami* are respected and honoured (through offerings and rituals) they can bring good luck, health and success.

In Shinto, purity and purification rituals are very important in both spiritual and secular life. It is believed that the human soul is born pure but can be corrupted later in life by anything that disrupts the natural order, including 'pollution' (events outside our control), sin (our own wrong actions) or, occasionally, bad *kami.* Purification rituals can take different forms but many involve hand washing.

Shinto is based entirely in the everyday world; there is no concept of another world and no goal of attaining salvation or a place in paradise. Shinto festivals celebrate the everyday events in our lives, such as the turning of the seasons or the day a person reaches adulthood. Ancestors are particularly revered and many families have small shrines in their homes to honour their ancestral *kami.*

TAKE A PURIFYING BATH

Shinto rituals use water or salt for purification, and the cleansing power of a salt bath is recommended by many for purifying not only the body (salt water draws toxins out of your tissues), but your aura too. Treat yourself to a ritual cleansing bath once a month. Use warm water (not too hot) with a couple of handfuls of unprocessed salt such as Himalayan rock salt. Light candles, play soothing music and wash away any negative thoughts.

RITUALS ARE
THE FORMULAS BY
WHICH HARMONY
IS RESTORED.

Terry Tempest
Williams

TO FORGET ONE'S
ANCESTORS IS TO BE A
BROOK WITHOUT SOURCE,
A TREE WITHOUT ROOT.

Chinese proverb

HONOUR YOUR ANCESTORS

Look into the lives of your ancestors and you will shed light not only on how you came to be where you are today, but also on who you are and what is important to you. You may want to set aside a corner of your home to display pictures of your ancestors, light a candle to remember them or add a vase of flowers as a token of gratitude for the gifts they have passed down to you.

SIKHISM

Sikhism, based on the teachings of Guru Nanak (1469–1539) and his nine successors, originated in the Punjab. Nanak felt that the rituals of other religions detracted from the pursuit of a relationship with God. He taught that actively doing good works – rather than carrying out rituals – was the most effective way of showing devotion to God.

Sikhs believe that humans cannot hope to understand God, but they can use ordinary life to get close to him, and can experience him through worship and contemplation. (Sikhism teaches that there is only one God for all religions.) By focusing on God in this way, Sikhs believe that they will ultimately be freed from the cycle of reincarnation.

Today, the emphasis of Sikhism is still very much on actively carrying out good works and benefitting the community, while keeping God in mind at all times. Sikhism has long been linked with a commitment to justice, and followers are taught to defend the defenceless and stand up to oppression.

A Sikh is expected to live honestly, be generous and treat others equally. The Sikh place of worship (the Gurdwara) is open to people of all faiths and is often the centre of the community. Decisions are made by the Sikh community as a group – there are no clergy – and men and women have equal status, making Sikhism a particularly egalitarian religion.

MAKE A STAND

There are times when we need to stand up for what we believe in. It can be difficult to voice our opinions if we are in the minority, but have the courage to speak your truth when it matters or you may regret not taking the opportunity once the moment has passed. And if you feel that someone else is being treated unfairly, or their voice is not being heard, lend them your support. Always follow your moral compass.

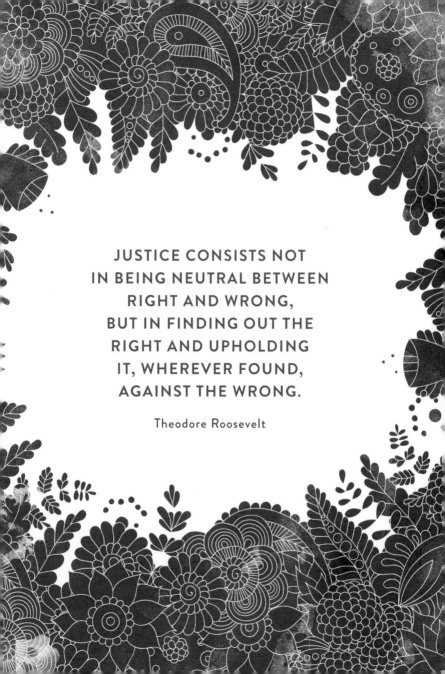

JUSTICE CONSISTS NOT
IN BEING NEUTRAL BETWEEN
RIGHT AND WRONG,
BUT IN FINDING OUT THE
RIGHT AND UPHOLDING
IT, WHEREVER FOUND,
AGAINST THE WRONG.

Theodore Roosevelt

AS FRAGRANCE
ABIDES IN THE FLOWER,
AS REFLECTION IS
WITHIN THE MIRROR,
SO DOES YOUR LORD
ABIDE WITHIN YOU.

Guru Nanak

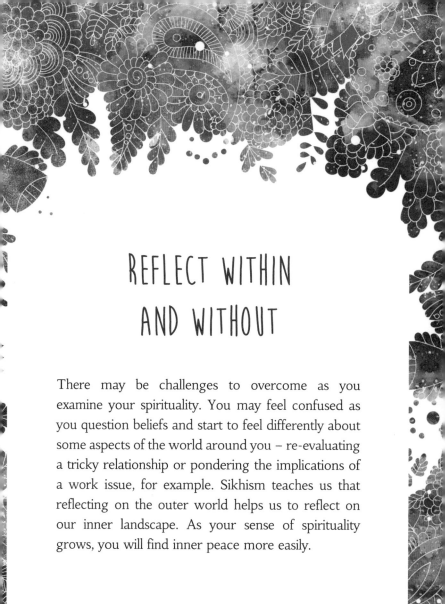

REFLECT WITHIN
AND WITHOUT

There may be challenges to overcome as you examine your spirituality. You may feel confused as you question beliefs and start to feel differently about some aspects of the world around you – re-evaluating a tricky relationship or pondering the implications of a work issue, for example. Sikhism teaches us that reflecting on the outer world helps us to reflect on our inner landscape. As your sense of spirituality grows, you will find inner peace more easily.

PICK POSITIVE PEOPLE

Surround yourself with people who motivate and encourage you and who make you feel good about yourself. Life is too short to spend time with those who drain us or who spread negative emotions, such as anger, sorrow and bitterness. When you're interacting with others, remember that the energy you give out has an effect on them too: make a conscious decision to have a positive influence on those around you and spread a little happiness.

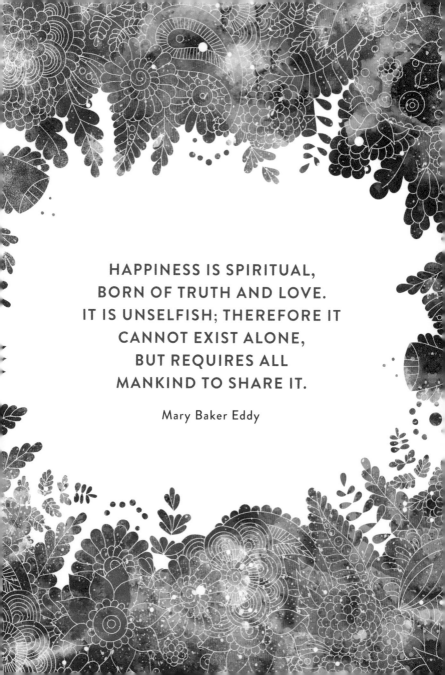

HAPPINESS IS SPIRITUAL,
BORN OF TRUTH AND LOVE.
IT IS UNSELFISH; THEREFORE IT
CANNOT EXIST ALONE,
BUT REQUIRES ALL
MANKIND TO SHARE IT.

Mary Baker Eddy

BAHÁ'Í

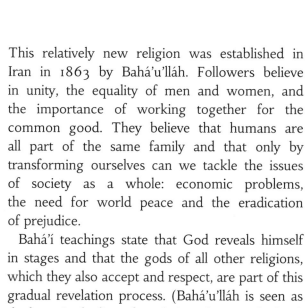

This relatively new religion was established in Iran in 1863 by Bahá'u'lláh. Followers believe in unity, the equality of men and women, and the importance of working together for the common good. They believe that humans are all part of the same family and that only by transforming ourselves can we tackle the issues of society as a whole: economic problems, the need for world peace and the eradication of prejudice.

Bahá'í teachings state that God reveals himself in stages and that the gods of all other religions, which they also accept and respect, are part of this gradual revelation process. (Bahá'u'lláh is seen as the latest in the line of revelations, but not the last.)

There are no clergy in the Bahá'í faith, but it is a spiritual path that must be walked in the company of others, who can encourage and advise as they travel together. The importance of family and of helping the wider community as a whole is also emphasised. Bahá'ís believe that they should work daily to improve themselves and that in doing so they are working towards the betterment of society – a principle that can inspire anyone on their spiritual journey.

LET YOUR VISION
BE WORLD-EMBRACING
RATHER THAN
CONFINED TO YOUR
OWN SELF.

Bahá'u'lláh

CONSIDER OTHERS

Recall those times you have been upset because someone let you down. Maybe they didn't meet you at an arranged time or they didn't call you when they told you they would. Now consider the times when you have done the same to others and make a promise to yourself that this will not happen again.

WHEN YOU ARE KIND
TO OTHERS IT NOT ONLY
CHANGES YOU, IT ALSO
CHANGES THE WORLD.

Harold Kushner

CARRY OUT RANDOM ACTS OF KINDNESS

Do something for others without expecting anything back – simple things, such as opening a door for someone, helping a colleague in the workplace or paying a compliment. There is no end to the random acts of kindness you can do every day that will cheer those around you. Set yourself a challenge and try to make three people happy every day!

FIND TIME
FOR FAMILY

It can be difficult to devote as much time to our families as we would like. Make an effort to call or visit a relative you haven't seen in a while, or organise a family get-together. You could try a new activity as a group or simply meet at a convenient spot for coffee and a chat – make it a regular event if you can. An hour now and then can be enough to strengthen family bonds.

FURTHER INFORMATION

GENERAL

Preston, David Lawrence *365 Steps to Practical Spirituality* (2007, How To Books)

Wilkinson, Tony *The Lost Art of Being Happy: Spirituality for Sceptics* (2007, Findhorn Press)

MINDFULNESS

Arnold, Dr Sarah Jane *The Mindfulness Companion* (2016, Michael O'Mara Books)

Collard, Dr Patrizia *The Little Book of Mindfulness* (2014, Gaia)

MEDITATION

Gauding, Madonna *The Meditation Bible* (2009, Godsfield Press)

Price, Sara Elliott *Meditation for Beginners* (2015, Amazon Media EU)

There are many good, guided meditations on YouTube. Search online for tried-and-tested favourites or visit www.chopra.com/ccl/guided-meditations

YOGA AND YOGIC BREATHING

Burgin, Timothy *Yoga for Beginners* (2012, AdhiMukti Press)

Hall, Jean *Breathe: Simple Breathing Techniques for a Calmer, Happier Life* (2016, Quadrille Publishing)

Isaacs, Nora *The Little Book of Yoga* (2014, Chronicle Books)

www.doyogawithme.com

www.yogajournal.com

CHANTING

Laron, Seth *Chanting: A Beginners' Guide to Using Meditation, Chanting and Mantras to Improve Your Health, Life and Wellbeing* (2015, Amazon Media EU)

Ray, Amit *Om Chanting and Meditation* (2010, Inner Light Publishers)

Experience chanting at home by searching online for free chanting tracks

LU JONG

Rinpoche, Tenzin *Healing with Form, Energy and Light* (2002, Snow Lion Publications)

www.lujong.org

QIGONG

Cohen, Kenneth *The Way of Qigong* (2000, Random House)

www.healthqigong.org.uk

T'AI CHI

Clark, Angus *Tai Chi: A Practical Approach to the Ancient Chinese Movement for Health and Well-being* (2002, Element)

Meredith, Scott *Tai Chi Peng Root Power Rising* (2014, Create Space)

www.taichiunion.com

AIKIDO

Brady, Peter *Aikido: Step by Step* (2013, Lorenz Books)

Francis, Dunken *Aikido: A Beginner's Guide* (2005, Wooden Dragon Press)

www.bab.org.uk

FASTING
Clear, Jonathan *Fasting: The Proven Practice for Weight Loss,*
Cleansing, Healing and Spiritual Growth
(2016, Amazon Media EU)
www.nhs.uk/Livewell/Healthyramadan/Pages/
fastingandhealth.aspx

CRYSTAL THERAPY
Hall, Judy *The Complete Crystal Workshop*
(2016, Godsfield Press)
Judith, Anodea *Chakras* (2016, Hay House)
www.therapy-directory.org.uk/articles/crystal-therapy.html
www.fht.org.uk/findatherapist

REIKI
McKenzie, Eleanor *Healing Reiki* (2005, Bounty Books)
McKenzie, Eleanor *The Reiki Bible* (2009, Godsfield Press)
www.reikiassociation.net

MODERN PAGANISM
Memory Paterson, Jacqueline *Tree Wisdom* (1996, Element)
van der Hoeven, Joanna *The Awen Alone*
(2014, Moon Books)
www.druidry.org

SHAMANISM
Kahili King, Serge *Urban Shaman* (1990, Simon & Schuster)
Sams, Jamie and Carson, David *Medicine Cards: the Discovery*
of Power Through the Ways of Animals
(1999, St Martin's Press)
Sentier, Elen *Shaman Pathways* (2013, Moon Books)
www.shamanlinks.net
www.spiritanimal.info

SPIRITUAL HEALING

Myss, Caroline *Anatomy of the Spirit* (1996, Bantam Books)
Ward, Tara *The Healing Handbook*
  (2000, Arcturus Publishing)

LAW OF ATTRACTION

Fletcher, Melody *Deliberate Receiving* (2015, Hay House)
MacDonald, Lucy *Learn to Be an Optimist* (2011, Watkins)

KARMA

Chodron, Thubten *Good Karma*
  (2016, Shambhala Publications)
Hamilton, Dr David *Why Kindness is Good for You*
  (2010, Hay House)
Kipfer, Barbara Ann *Instant Karma*
  (2003, Workman Publishing)

THEOSOPHY

Christie, Catherine W. *Theosophy for Beginners*
  (1910, new edition 2016, Square Circles Publishing)
The Theosophy Trust, *Theosophy: The Wisdom Religion*
  (2015, Theosophy Trust Books)
www.theosophical.org

HINDUISM

Achuthananda, Swami *Many Many Many Gods of Hinduism*
  (2013, Create Space)
Knott, Kim *Hinduism: A Very Short Introduction* (2000, OUP)
www.hinducounciluk.org

BUDDHISM

Barry, Dylan *Zen Buddhism* (2014, Happy Dhamma)
Brahm, Ajahn *Opening the Door of Your Heart*
  (2015, Hachette Australia)
Thích Nhất Hạnh, *Peace is Every Step* (1991, Bantam Books)
www.thebuddhistsociety.org

JAINISM

Jaini, Jagmanderlal *Outlines of Jainism*
  (2013, Cambridge University Press)
Long, Jeffery D. *Jainism: An Introduction*
  (2009, I. B. Tauris & Co.)
www.jainology.org

CONFUCIANISM

Confucius, *The Analects* (1979, Penguin Classics)

SHINTO

Yamakage, Motohisa *The Essence of Shinto*
  (2012, Kodansha America)
Reader, Ian *Shinto* (1998, Simple Guides)

SIKHISM

Cole, Owen *Sikhism: An Introduction* (2010, Teach Yourself)
Mandair, Arvind-Pal Singh *Sikhism: A Guide for the Perplexed*
  (2013, Bloomsbury)
www.sikhs.org

BAHA'I

Momen, Moojan *A Short Introduction to the Baha'i Faith*
  (1997, Oneworld)
www.bahai.org.uk

Have you enjoyed this book?
If so, why not write a review on
your favourite website?

If you're interested in finding out more
about our books, find us on Facebook
at **Summersdale Publishers** and follow us
on Twitter at **@Summersdale**.

Thanks very much for buying
this Summersdale book.

www.summersdale.com